HOW DO SCIENTISTS DISCOVER NEW PLANETS?

ASTRONOMY BOOK 2ND GRADE

Children's Astronomy & Space Books

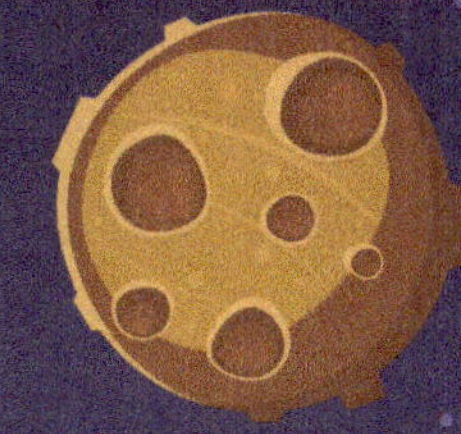

In this book, we're going to talk about how scientists discover new planets. So, let's get right to it!

Until about 30 years ago, astronomers didn't know if there were any systems of planets outside our solar system. The idea that there could be other planets orbiting stars far outside our own galaxy had been talked about in science fiction but wasn't yet a science fact. Then, in 1988, the very first exoplanet was discovered!

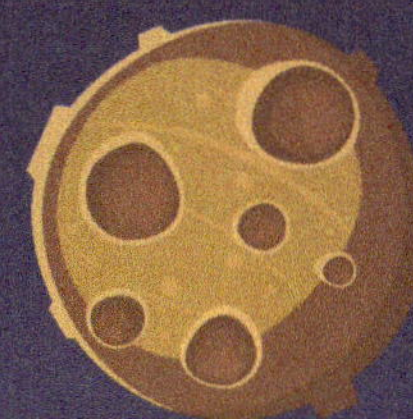

Extrasolar planets or exoplanets

WHAT IS AN EXOPLANET?

Distant planet system in space 3D rendering Elements of this image furnished by NASA

An exoplanet is a planet that is outside our solar system and orbits a star that is not our sun. After the first exoplanet was discovered, it was only a matter of time until astronomers perfected their methods for finding exoplanets. Today, astronomers have data on over 1,700 exoplanets.

View of an exoplanet from space during a sunrise.
'elements of this image furnished by NASA'

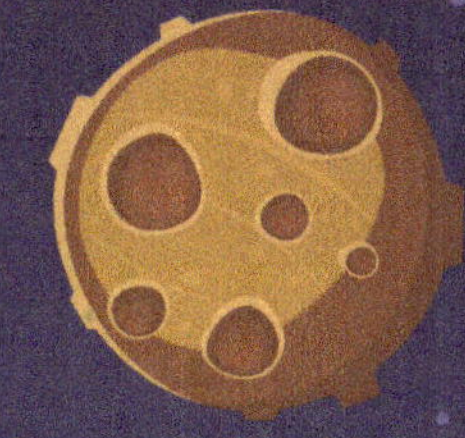

Some are huge planets that have orbits very close to their stars. Some are rocky and some have icy surfaces. Some of them travel around two stars instead of just one. There are even some exoplanets that astronomers believe are filled with water.

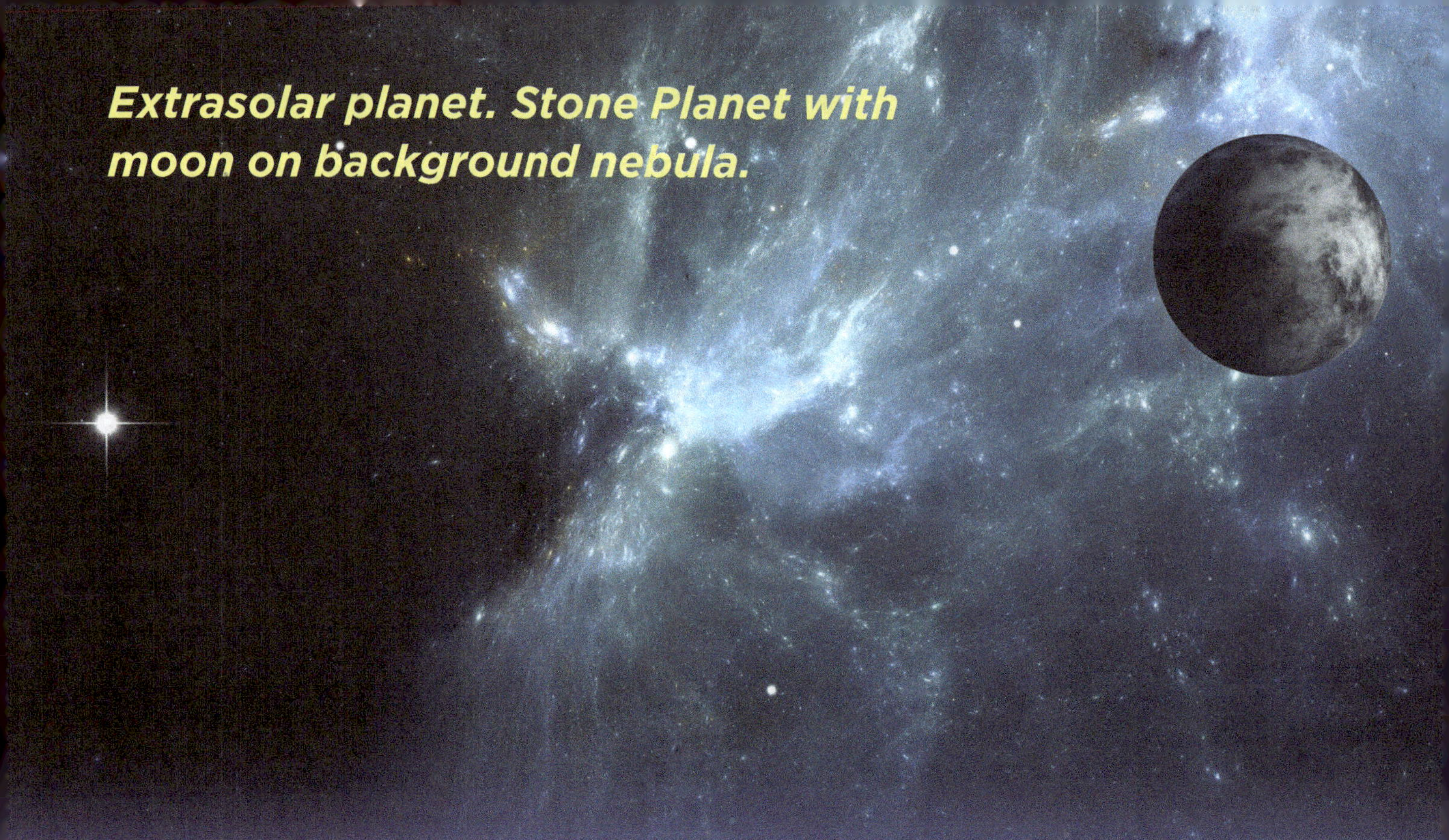

Extrasolar planet. Stone Planet with moon on background nebula.

There are some that are the size of Earth and others that are two times the size of Jupiter, which is the largest planet in our solar system. In fact, so many planets have been found, that NASA scientists

are classifying some of them based on how similar they are to Earth. Most of the planets have been found because of data sent by the Kepler Space Telescope, which was sent out to space in 2009.

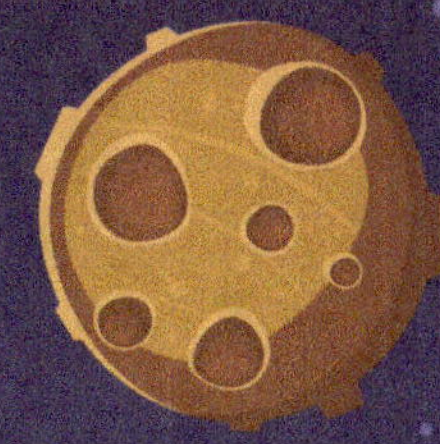

There is one thing that all these planets have in common. At this point, almost all of them are too far away to be seen even with the assistance of our most powerful telescopes.

Since the first exoplanet was found, scientists have been working on ways to find these planets. Sometimes they use more than one method to confirm their findings after an exoplanet has been discovered.

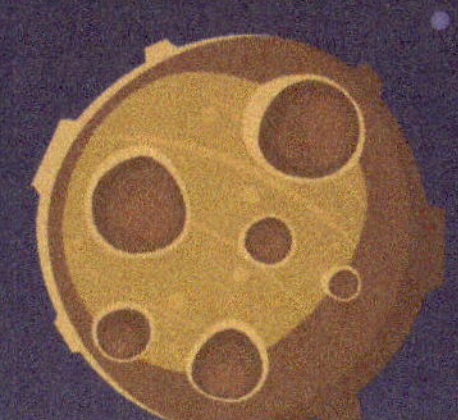

3D render of unreal Trappist-1 exoplanets system

Our Planet
Hunting
Neighborhood
Sun
90% of planets with
known distances lie
within about 2000
light-years from our
Sun, as of July 2014.

THE TRANSIT METHOD

Imagine that a friend is holding a lamp in front of you. Then a second friend holds up a basketball between your line of sight and the lamp. The lamp's light can't totally get to you now because the basketball is blocking it. This is basically the method that astronomers are using when they use the transit method.

As a planet rotates around its star in a regular pattern, there are times when it will be between the Kepler Telescope and its star. During those times, the amount of brightness of the star takes a dip because the planet is passing in front of it. By measuring this data, astronomers can tell whether there's a planet there or not.

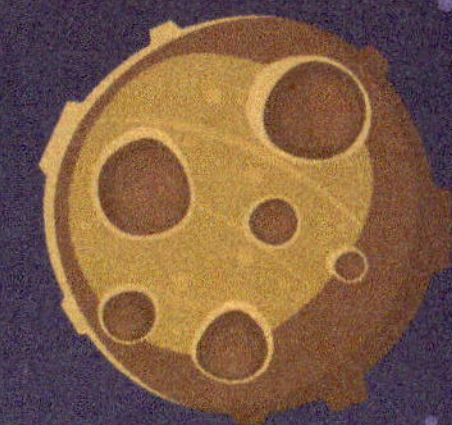

Map of Exoplanets Found in Our Galaxy (Artist's Concept)

Artist's conception of a simultaneous transit of three planets before Kepler-11 observed by NASA's Kepler spacecraft on Aug. 26, 2010.

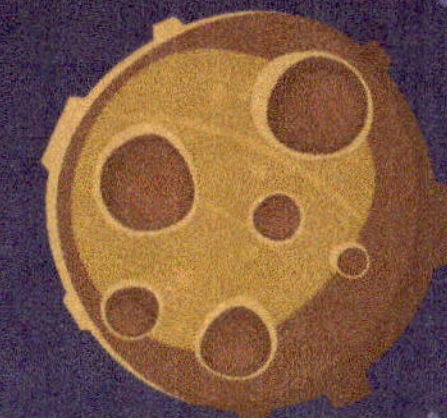

Depending on how much the brightness of the star dims, astronomers can sometimes tell how big the planet is. Suppose they know the star's size and how far the planet is from its star. With those measurements, once they figure out the change in brightness, they can figure out how big the planet's radius is.

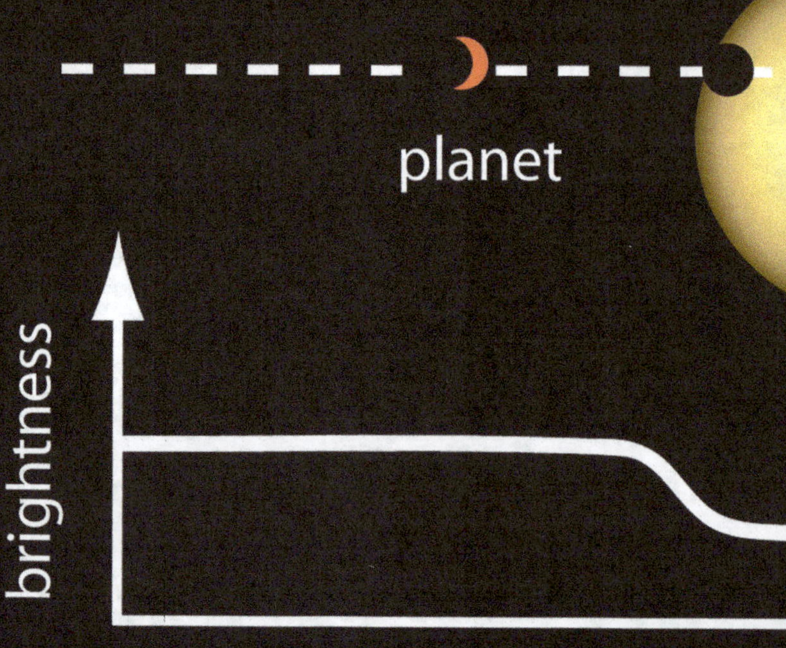

Unfortunately, there are some problems with this method. A planet needs to be lined up a certain way to pass between our telescope and its star. The farther away the planet is, the less chance there is that our telescope and the planet are in the correct position at the same time. If there

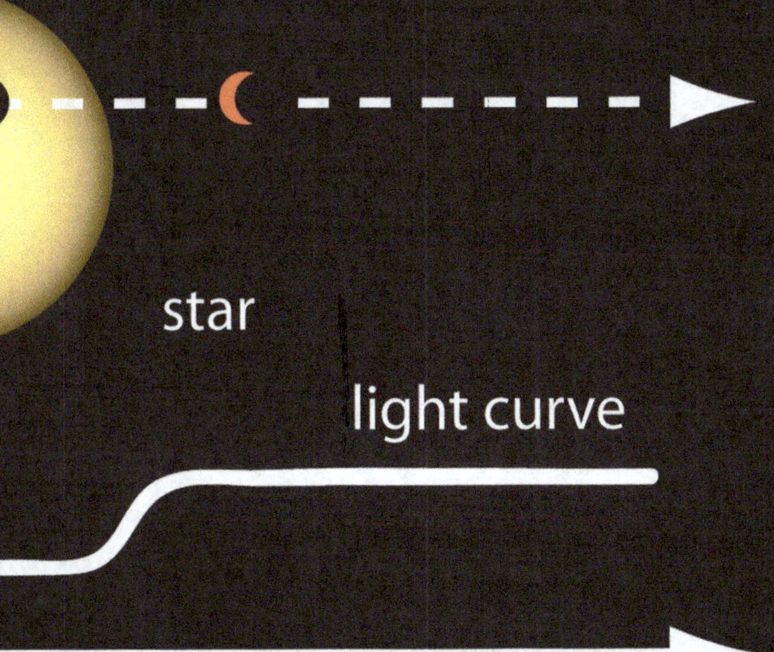

was a planet that was the size of Earth, orbiting at the same distance that ours does, there's only a 0.5 percent chance that it would be lined up properly to cause a change in the star's brightness.

Seeing planets using the Transit Method.

Shown is an illustration of Kepler 62e, about 1,200 light-years away in the constellation Lyra. Image by NASA.

Because of this, there is a lot of data that astronomers are studying that could be incorrect. The dimming that is caused could be dust or something else that is causing the star to appear dimmer. Since there could be so many errors, astronomers use other methods to check their results once they find an exoplanet using the transit method.

THE ORBITAL BRIGHTNESS METHOD

Surprisingly, sometimes a planet causes the amount of light from a star to be brighter instead of dimmer. This happens when the planet travels very close to its star.

Hot Jupiters, exoplanets around the same size as Jupiter that orbit very closely to their stars, often have cloud or haze layers in their atmospheres. Image by NASA.

Artist's concept of a rocky Earth-sized exoplanet in the habitable zone of its host star, possibly compatible with Kepler-452b's known data.

The planet gets heated up, and then we detect more brightness from the heat radiation, which is called thermal radiation. The change in brightness happens on a regular basis and even though the astronomers can't see the planet, they suspect that it's there, because the brightness changes have a pattern.

If the planet is in the right alignment, its data reveals something like the phases of the moon. It waxes and wanes in terms of brightness. Just a few exoplanets have been found this way so far, but this method may be used more in the future because it doesn't have the same problems with it as the transit method does.

Artist's impression of a transiting Jupiter-mass exoplanet SWEEPS.

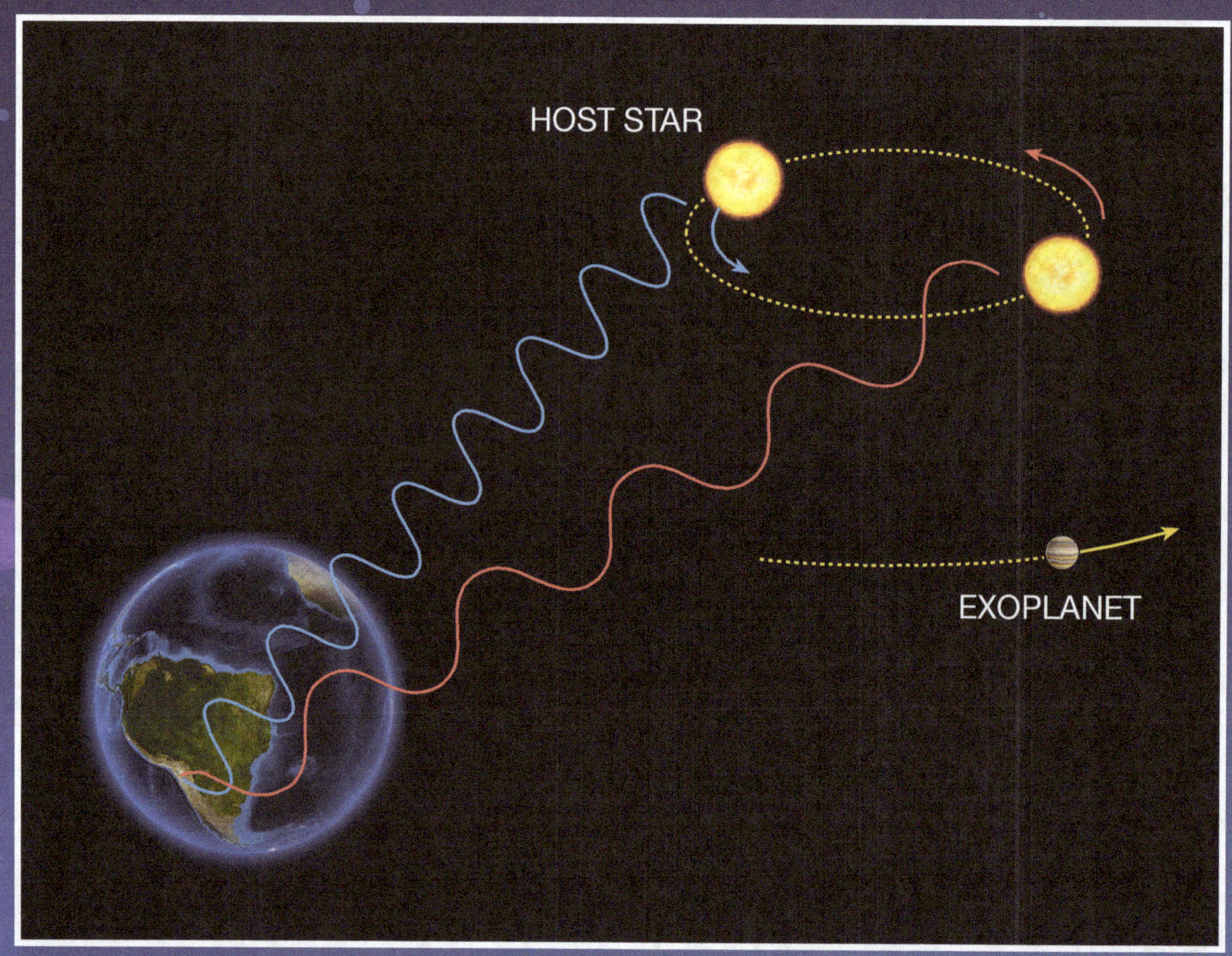

The Radial Velocity Method.
ESO Press Photo 22e/07

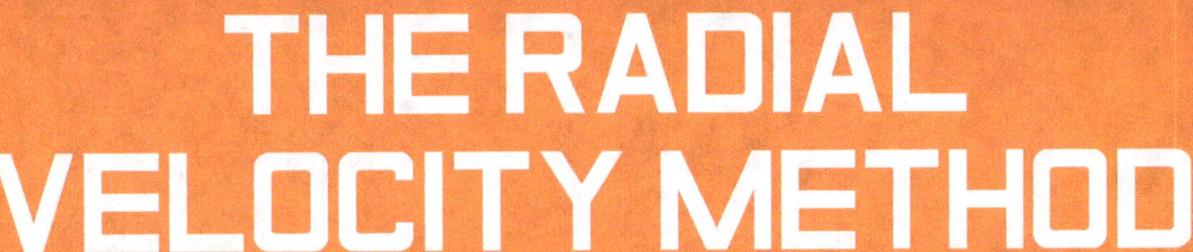

THE RADIAL VELOCITY METHOD

The first time you learn about the solar system, it sounds like our sun always stays in the same exact spot and that everything, such as planets and asteroids revolve around it. However, that's not exactly true. The gravity of very large planets does affect their stars. It causes them to wobble ever so slightly from the center of gravity of the system.

If a large planet is big enough and close enough, it pulls its star a little and this causes the star to wobble a little away from the center of its system. Astronomers can use these tiny shifts in the position of the star to come to the conclusion that there is a big planet orbiting that particular star.

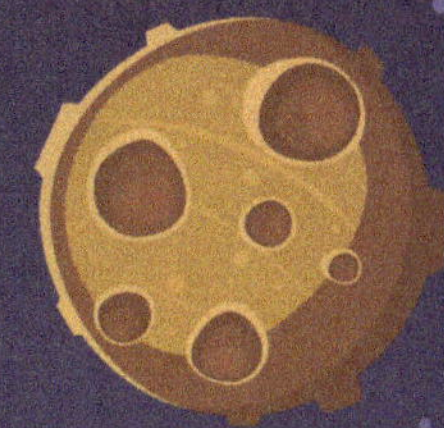

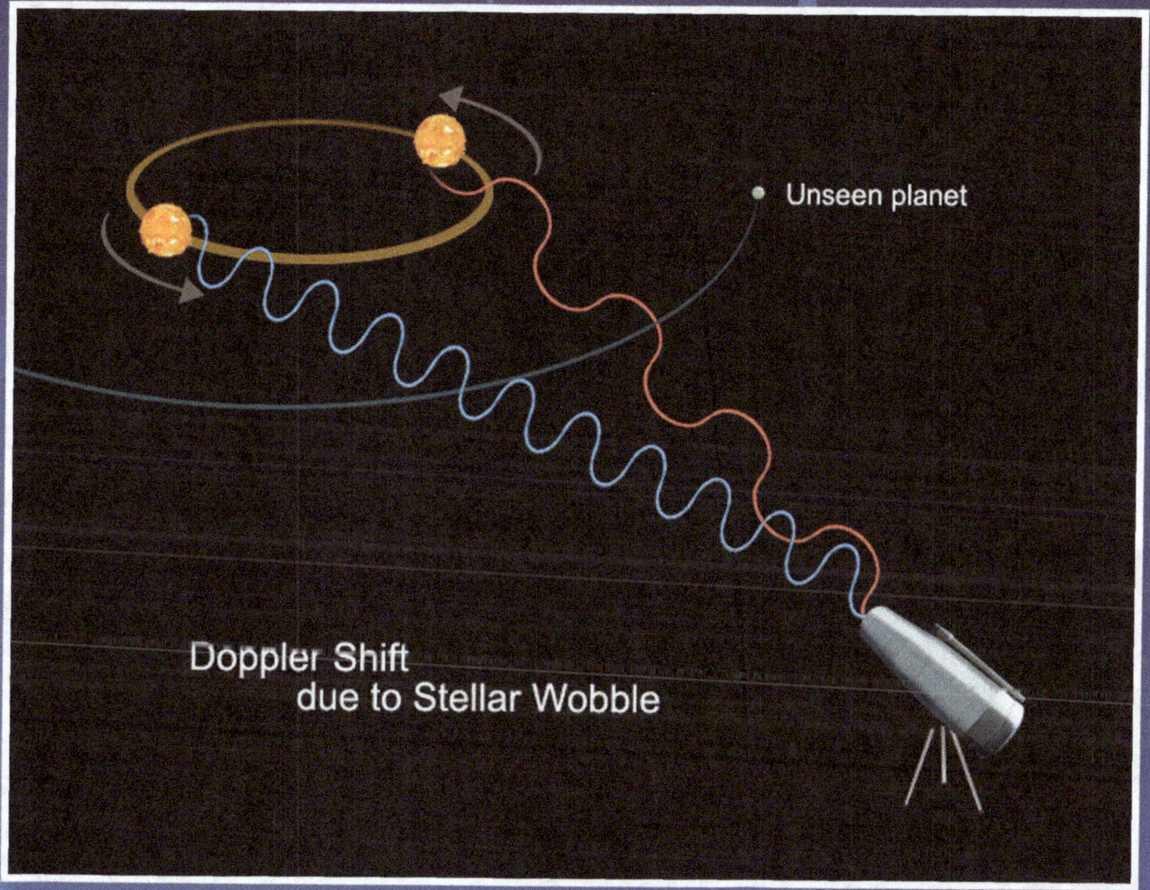

This illustration demonstrates the "wobble," or radial velocity, technique for finding planets.

It seems impossible that astronomers could measure these tiny wobbles in stars that are huge distances away, but they can. The reason is something called

er-452b

Kepler-62f

Kepler-186f

Earth

the Doppler effect. They can tell when a star is moving quickly away from Earth or quickly toward Earth at distances of about one meter for every second.

If you've heard an ambulance before, then you've experienced the Doppler effect. When an ambulance is driving toward you, it has a high-pitched sound. When it drives away that sound is the same, but it sounds lower in tone as the ambulance drives off.

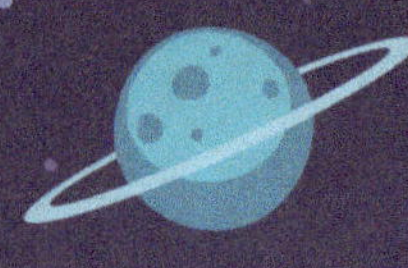

Kepler's newest planetary find joins a pantheon of planets with similarities to Earth.
Image by NASA

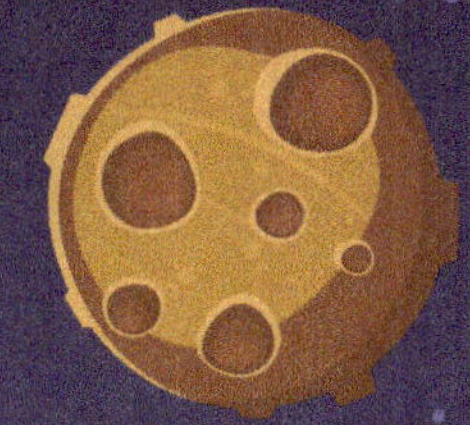

Waves, whether they are sound, light, or other types of energy, seem to have a higher frequency when the object is headed toward the observer. These same waves seem to have a lower frequency when the waves are moving away from the observer. This is similar to how astronomers measure the shift in the star's light based on whether its location is either headed toward or headed away.

Astronomers use a special device called a spectrometer to measure the frequency of a star's light. By measuring these shifts, they can tell the direction that the star is moving. The amount of movement can even tell them something about the planet's mass.

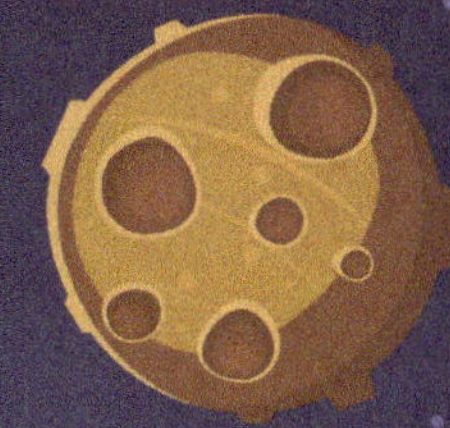

HARPS spectrograph.

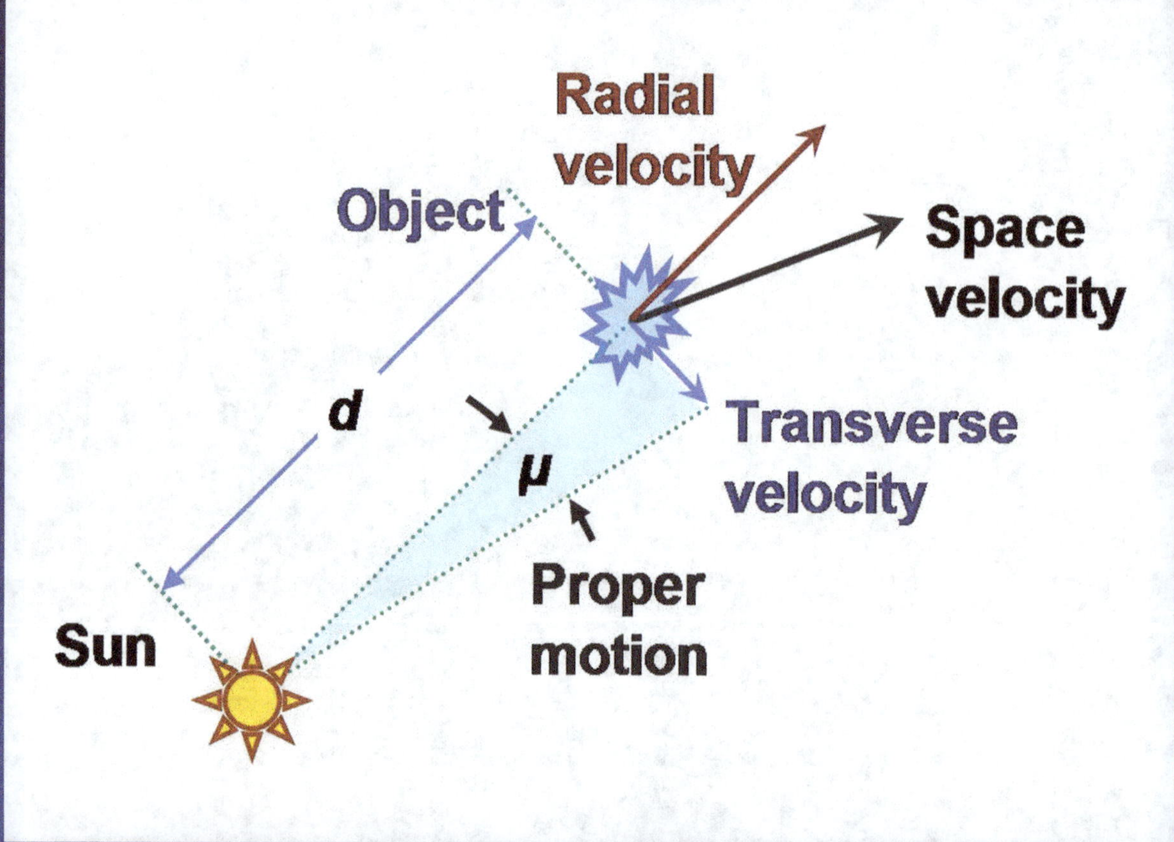

Diagram showing relation between an object's proper motion and its velocity.

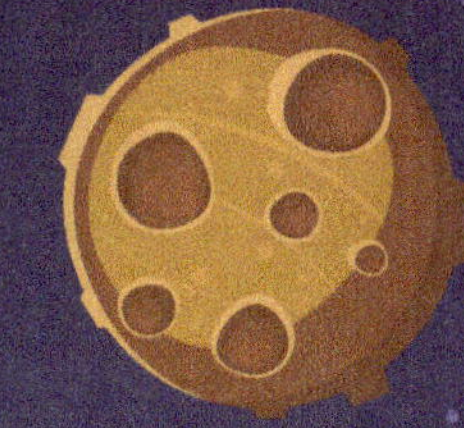

If they combine it with the transit method, they may be able to find the radius of the planet. Once they have the mass and radius, they can compute the density. A dense planet might be rocky like Earth. One that's less dense might be made up of gas.

This method works best at finding big planets that are orbiting around smaller stars. The reason is that the planet has more of a pull on the star. Planets that are smaller or mid-sized like Earth would be harder to find using this method.

In the search for distant worlds, few telescopes have had as much success as ESO's 3.6-metre telescope and the Swiss 1.2-metre Leonhard Euler Telescope, both of which are shown in this image. The 3.6-metre telescope is home to HARPS (High Accuracy Radial velocity Planet Searcher), a spectrograph with unrivalled precision.

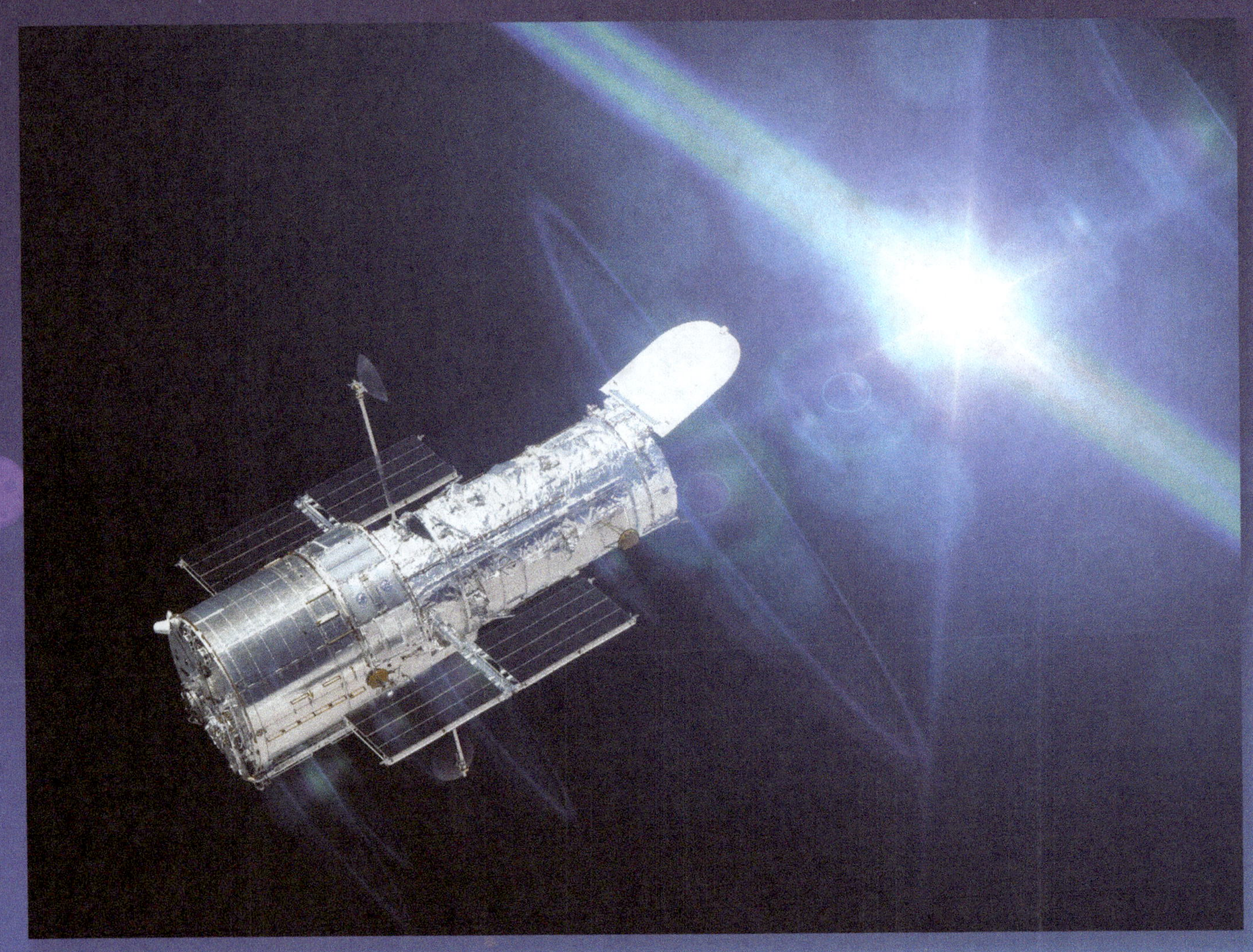

Hubble Space Telescope observing a star.
(3D illustration, elements of this image are by NASA)

THE DIRECT IMAGING METHOD

There have been a few cases when astronomers have found an exoplanet by seeing it with a space telescope. There are reasons that these cases are rare. The light from stars is generally very bright so at a distance it's hard to distinguish a close planet from its star.

For example, imagine if you were trying to see the small planet Mercury, which is close to the sun, while you were looking at the sun from outside our solar system. On the other hand, if the planet is too far away from its star, it might not reflect enough light to be seen at all.

Observatory dome at the peak of Mauna Kea volcano, Hawaii.

This Illustreation shows the closest known planetary system to our own, called Epsilon Eridani.

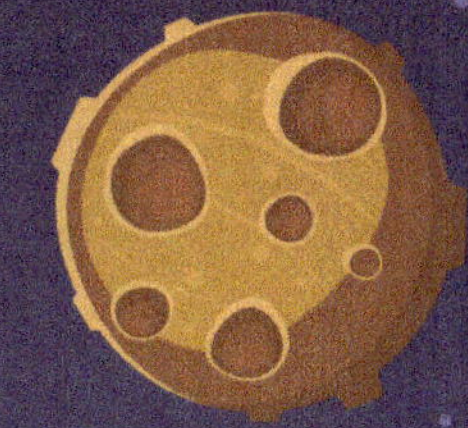

The exoplanets that have been found through viewing with telescopes have been very large like our planet Jupiter. They've also been very hot and their heat can be detected by telescopes. Planets that travel around brown dwarfs, which are bodies that don't give off much light, can also be seen more easily.

THE GRAVITATIONAL LENSING METHOD

Think about a star that is way, way out in space. Another star is about half the distance between the far away star and Earth. Even though they are light years apart, they may line up at rare times when they are being viewed in the night sky. When this happens, the gravity of the

Artist's Impression of the 10 hot Jupiter exoplanets.

closer star is similar to a telescope. It magnifies the light from the distant star so we can see it better.

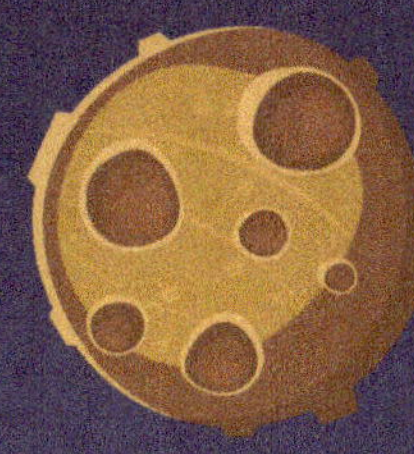

If the star nearest to our view has a planet, the planet's gravity makes the lens a little more magnified. When astronomers measure this, they know that the star that's closer has a planet moving around it. They can tell that there's a planet there, by the way it magnifies the light of a star that's even further away!

Awesome! Now you know more about the five ways that scientists discover new planets. You can find more Astronomy & Space books from Baby Professor by searching the website of your favorite book retailer.

Exoplanet - extrasolar planet in distant solar system in outer space.

Visit

BABY PROFESSOR
EDUCATION KIDS

www.BabyProfessorBooks.com

to download Free Baby Professor eBooks
and view our catalog of new and exciting
Children's Books